THE ARCHITECTURE OF MEXICO

YESTERDAY AND TODAY

The
Architecture
of MEXICO

Yesterday and Today

By HANS BEACHAM

Introduction by Mathias Goeritz

ARCHITECTURAL BOOK PUBLISHING COMPANY

New York 10016

FRONTISPIECE: A Franciscan building of typical simplicity, the sixteenth-century Church of Santiago stands
symbolically between the pre-Hispanic ruins of Tlatelolco
and the modern apartment buildings designed recently
by Mario Pani.

PICTURE CREDITS: Photographs on pages 32-35, 40 (upper), 110, 170-175, 224-225 and 252-253 were made by
Guillermo Zamora. All other illustrations were made by
the author.

OPPOSITE PAGE: Decorative detail from a Guanajuato
house shown on pages 206-215.

Copyright © 1969
by Architectural Book Publishing Co., Inc.

Published simultaneously in Canada by
Saunders, of Toronto, Ltd. Don Mills, Ontario

SBN: 8038-0013-4
Library of Congress Catalog Card Number: 69-15058
Printed in the United States of America

CONTENTS

LEFT: Architect Juan José Díaz Infante designed this plastic structure as a partial solution to Mexico's housing problem. BELOW: Dewdrops cling to a type of plastic webbing that is rapidly replacing natural fibers in furniture and basket weaving. OPPOSITE PAGE: Traditional materials, adobe and plaster, lend a contemporary effect to a utility building at the public swimming pools in Atotonilco, Morelos.

INTRODUCTION

IN this country of Mexico the contrasts of old and new are placed abruptly together, one against the other. The placement is made without hesitation, without compassion. There are few countries in which the old is so brilliantly old, or where the new is so brilliantly new. Generally, in European countries old traditions smother what is new while in those countries that are young the modern world causes a renunciation of the past. But the Mexicans are architectural contrapuntists — theirs is a strange and foreign harmony, a counterpoint of ancient and modern.

This is the harmony one feels when one comes upon a sixteenth-century convent placed alongside a pyramid or when one discovers "windows a Go-Go" in a baroque cathedral. The melody comes from young people who are intensely involved with today. It does *not* come from those timid souls who want simply to reconstruct the past — old yesterdays — in an effort to avoid a confrontation with the philosophic demands of today. Mexico is not a petit bourgeois, guarding a little porcelain cup simply because it belonged to an old grandmother. On the contrary, it is a country that most generously recognizes what is simply excellent. Could it be that the extraordinary

Mexican landscape itself formed the people it contains? I do not know; but I do know that the goodness of these people is reflected in the dimensions of their work, in the spaces formed by their architecture and in the rich variety of all their arts.

The forcing together of varied forms and ideas, along with their expression in styles and techniques completely unrelated to each other, results in a paradoxical unity that would be simply impossible in any other culture. In Mexico, a paradox is feasible. The Mexican artistic forms must follow their own special laws of integration, distinct from those of other latitudes, because all elements, ancient and modern, seem to be active.

For one thing, the fascinated observer can see to what extent the ancient survives through the popular traditions that persist today. On the other hand, it is rightly so that the grass-roots culture of Mexico, as it exists today, is solidly based on the inexhaustible heritage of its past. Each sustains the other. A profound sense of mysticism and a religiosity almost pagan are prime forces in this esthetic survival that has its roots in the pre-Cortesian world. And while the Revolution was able to change the social structure of the country and the conditions of life — material and intellectual — it did not alter the character of the men who made the Revolution.

OPPOSITE: Detail from the famous mosaics at Mitla, Oaxaca, where cut stones were joined so perfectly that mortar was unnecessary.

The younger generations came, and with them was born a world of new ideas that had nothing in common with tradition except its zealous concern for integrity. *Do not make concessions! Be of your own epoch! This is how you create YOUR way!*

This is not to say that deep relationships do not always exist between the world of yesterday and the worlds of today and tomorrow. The character of the past addresses us today; it prevails through forms. They turn up in architecture that uses the same elemental triangles, cones and pyramids; the same juxtaposition of primary forms; the same baroque exuberance; the same preference for certain materials; the same marvelous feeling for the monumental.

The contemporary architects, along with other artists, do not deny the treasure of the past, so rich, and richer than any other. They admire it, but they continue forward. And what happens? The newest international experiences get launched in Mexico but, without specifically intending to, the architects convert internationalism into a typical Mexican manifestation. On the other hand, those individuals who want conscientiously to follow the formal traditions will arrive, in spite of themselves, to utilize the forms and embellishments which are either popular or ancient, resulting again in something typically Mexican.

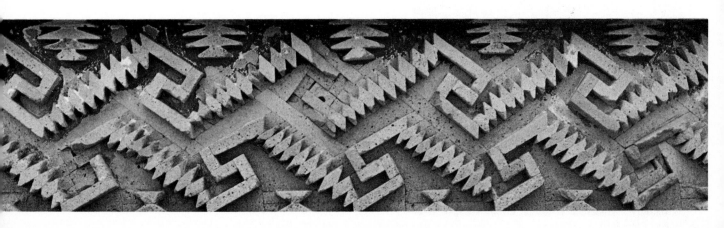

Attracted by the richness of these distinctive civilizations and their plastic expressions, Hans Beacham proposes to show the complexity of Mexico's architectural art in the photographs of this book. For some two decades now he has been actively occupied with the theme "Mexico." He has dealt with this idea most especially in the photographs he has made of Mexico's most outstanding artists and intellectuals. From such a vantage point the sensitive foreigner gains a privileged entry into the real structure of Mexican life. In effect, Beacham has enjoyed a position from which he could see everything. (Writing about him in *Excelsior*, the late Margarita Nelkin once observed that he was a psychiatrist who did his analysis with a camera.) But having done so well in an area where subjectivity is almost a prerequisite, he has had to reverse his methods in the project at hand. A confrontation with architecture and its related art forms is an entirely different discipline, in which the photographer must suppress himself stylistically so that the subject itself may be communicated with as little "art" as possible. But being an artist himself, Beacham still leaves his personal stamp on this work because of the material he selected and the way he has put it together.

Beacham has an eye that is analytic but also romantic. These attributes, combined with a subtle sense of irony, have always controlled the camera

Carved detail from an early Porfirian-styled door in Londres Street, Mexico City.

he uses. In this project he was wise to yield all but the essence of his own personality. He had the valor to approach the theme with an extraordinary sense of justice, which at the same time prevented him from falling into the obvious or the easy. In a few cases, when he was unable to capture what he wanted with his own camera he simply commissioned another photographer, which is certainly an act of modesty. In choosing from the thousands of his own photographs, Beacham eliminated many because they were more beautiful than informative. The happy consequence is that neither photography for its own sake nor the photographer himself has obstructed the subject-matter. He used illustrations that would represent his impartial viewpoint, in juxtaposition to a theme that, in another person's hands, might have seemed mannered or flippant.

If I were a photographer and had been assigned the task that Beacham has done, this book doubtless would have come out very different. But I believe, I confess, that it would not have been as interesting, nor as profound, nor as beautiful.

Mathias Goeritz

OLD AND NEW

NEARLY twenty years ago, during a rainstorm in the Isthmus of Tehuantepec, we were invited to take shelter and refreshments with an old shepherd and his wife. His thatched hut was warm, dry and impeccably clean. On one wall hung a small plaster statute of the Virgin, painted pink and blue. Illuminated by a candle, she was standing on a half-moon. To her left hung a bright chromium-plated hubcap from a 1935 Plymouth. The combination, though startling, did not seem incorrect. Today these improbable decorative juxtapositions are still startling but also continue to seem correct. This is because the foreigner can rarely become jaded in Mexico. In fact, he is in danger of *expecting* to be surprised at every turn. Such an attitude would limit his point of view and do the Mexicans an injustice.

The subjects of the work at hand deserve to be shown not trickily but as directly as possible. Until the unlikely time when buildings are able to photograph themselves, however, an author's declared aim may differ from the result. If I err, sentiment, not technique, will have been responsible. The problem has been not *how* to show something, but rather *why*. What results is a considerable cross-section of Mexican architecture. The prevalence and persistence of a certain style, rather than my personal tastes, determine how much space that style receives below. Baroque, for example, gets much more coverage than neo-classical; modern gets only slightly less than baroque.

As this study grew, a certain paradox began to emerge; what is new in Mexican architecture may often seem ancient, even pre-Hispanic; what is old, even pre-Hispanic, may often seem surprisingly contemporary.

OPPOSITE PAGE: In downtown Mexico City, at the corners of Madero and San Juan de Letran streets, Dr. Leonardo Zeevaert's Latin American Tower building has become a national symbol of modern Mexican architecture. The conventional church in the foreground faces Madero Street.

OPPOSITE PAGE: The new Aztec Stadium — steel, cement and aluminum — is a great public theater seating more than 100,000 spectators. BELOW: Relic of another era, this small private theater in Real de Catorce, San Luis Potosí, presented cockfighting to an audience of two hundred. PAGES 16-17: Reminiscent of a drawing by Rowland Emett, these black iron towers at Mexico City's old Museum of National History contrast sharply with the present direction in non-functional architecture. The cement towers, designed by Mathias Goeritz in collaboration with Luis Barragán, stand at the entrance of Satellite City, a project planned by Mario Pani.

The churrígueresque Church of San Francisco Xavier at Tepotzotlan, State of Mexico, finished in 1682, has been restored several times. Now a public museum, the building houses fine examples of decorative art from the seventeenth and eighteenth centuries. The nave, appropriately decorated, serves as a theater for concerts of baroque music. Built by Jesuits, the church features their patron Saint Ignatius Loyola (*below, left*) in the decorations. The Archangel Michael appears in the other detail.

Alejandro Zohn designed this Protestant Chapel in Guadalajara. Using basic materials and avoiding decorative embellishments, Zohn has achieved the quiet, spiritual atmosphere appropriate to a place of worship.

ABOVE: When land was plentiful, before the time of elevators and structural steel, office buildings like the National Palace spread horizontally, covering city blocks. LEFT: Today, of course, construction is nearly always perpendicular, like this new Guadalajara office building designed by Julio de la Peña.

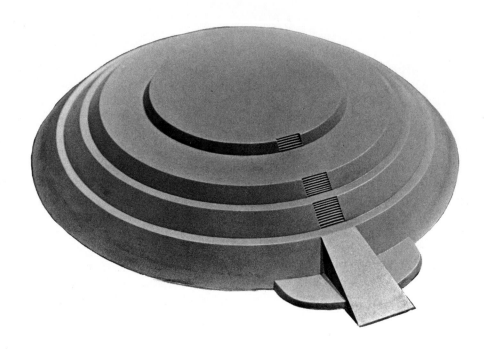

Above is a model of the pyramid of Cuicuilco from Mexico City's National Museum of Anthropology. The actual ruins, shown below, are just outside Mexico City, not far from the National University. Although there is still argument about Cuicuilco's earliest dates, C-14 tests suggest a date of about 800 B.C. A local volcano, Xitla, put an end to the settlement around 300 A.D. The substructure at Cuicuilco is 387 feet in diameter. Four additional tiers, each progressively smaller, rise seventy-five feet. Filled with sand and rubble, the structure is faced with rocks. Other ancient structures were found nearby when a site was being prepared for the 1968 Olympics.

PYRAMIDS, CONES AND TRIANGLES

MAN's earliest architectural creations of any grandeur often appeared as pyramids. In Mexico they began as platforms faced with sun-dried clay. As hierarchical societies developed, the structures acquired sloping walls of field stone, often plastered and painted. Religion inspired them and a ruling priest unified the community. The pyramid and all its related shapes occur in nature, thanks to the normal processes of erosion or to nascent volcanoes. As an architectural form the eminently functional pyramid fulfills man's desire for precision and order. Further, in ancient Mexico the fire god Xiutecuhtli was lord of all the volcanoes. He seems to have been one of the earliest inspirations to builders in pre-Hispanic Mexico; his likeness, usually in the form of incense burners, has been unearthed from beneath the lava flows of the Pedregal.

In Egypt the solid stone pyramids served as tombs to perpetuate men who had become gods but in Mexico only one pyramid is known to have contained a tomb. Mexican pyramids, therefore, largely reflect the spirit of the people rather than the individual. Inspired by many deities, these pyramids stemmed from nature and the gods she implied. Today that intrepid descendent of the pyramid, the hip roof, continues to give distinguished service in rainy climates.

BELOW: These new *trojes*, or granaries, conical in design, are near Pedro Escobedo, Querétaro. OPPOSITE PAGE: (*Top*) Pyramid of the Moon in the pre-Hispanic city of Teotihuacan, dating from the archaic period. The style shown here is the classic, which flourished between the fourth and ninth centuries A.D. (*Middle*) The modified triangular shapes of the façade of the Tri-Ply factory in Oaxaca harmonize with the diamond-shaped embellishments formed by the roof of the building in the right background. (*Bottom*) In designing the ball courts at Mexico's National University, architect Arai used basic pyramidal shapes harmonizing with surrounding mountains. The black stone came from ancient lava flows abounding in the area.

BELOW: Not far from the ball courts (page 26) is a spectator stand, with utility rooms below, which echoes Arai's basic design. Bleachers on the roof overlook the University's swimming pool. OPPOSITE: The Monument to the Race (*Bottom*) has existed in several forms. With recently installed pipes and nozzles, it is now a fountain in one of Mexico City's elaborate traffic complexes. In the right background appears the tower shown close-up on the following page. (*Above*) A triangular base of cast cement for a flagpole, located near Teotihuacan.

This pyramidal office building, left, has become a trademark of the urban development at Tlatelolco. The sloping sides are faced with tiny ceramic tiles that from a distance appear to be terrazzo. Close by, at right, a low, horizontal building is supported by iron beams inclined to 45° and crossing each other at right angles to form a series of triangles. These repeat the lines of the steps in the foreground, which Aztec priests once ascended to supervise the ancient sacrificial rites of Tlatelolco.

A view of the ruins at Monte Alban, Oaxaca.

Though technically modern in every respect, in design these Social Security buildings in Villahermosa, Tabasco, descend from Monte Alban and the Mayan cities of Yucatán. Designed by Salvador Ortega, the buildings were finished in 1967.

An interior view showing the main lobby of the Social Security complex at Villa-hermosa. Note the lavish use of small round stones, inside and out, as a practical wall facing.

Another view, made from an inner court, showing a massive pyramidal wall faced with stone mosaic. This kind of facing was used in ancient Mexico.

ARCHITECTURE AND RELIGION

No student of Mexican architecture old and new need be disquieted to discover that a considerable proportion of his investigation must deal with architecture inspired by religion. As a work like Anita Brenner's *Idols Behind Altars* indicates, building to the glory of God or the gods was a continuous process uninterrupted by conquests, Spanish or internecine.

Like the ceremonial cross on the facing page, Mexican religious architecture can often be a startling combination of design elements. This is especially true of decorative detail. In the most modern churches, like those designed by Candela or de la Mora, decoration is minimal. This is the latest expression in the evolution of religious architecture itself.

Opposite Page: Early nineteenth-century ceremonial cross from Guanajuato. Notice the pre-Hispanic sun and moon at Christ's fingertips. Below him are persons in purgatory. This type of cross is still used extensively in many villages in the states of Guanajuato and Querétaro. (*From the collection of Prof. Willis W. Pratt.*)

Esthetically the Pyramid of the Niches at Tajín is one of the most satisfying to be found anywhere. It is a relatively small pyramid, less than sixty feet tall, but its perfect symmetry, its intricate step-and-fret embellishments and its facing of carved stone blocks are among the finest examples of pre-Hispanic art. Building techniques at Tajín were sophisticated. Nearby structures, probably royal residences, had roofs made from poured concrete slabs. The inhabitants wrote and counted with glyphs and bar-and-dot numbers. The pyramid shown here has 365 niches, one for each day of the solar year.

The religion of this civilization involved ball games, human sacrifice and an omnipresent death god who appears in relief and sculpture on most of the buildings. Below, he is seen descending to claim a victim being sacrificed by the winners of a ball game.

The Pyramid of the Niches achieved its present design sometime between the sixth and eighth centuries A.D. but was superimposed upon another smaller pyramid of similar design that may date from the first century B.C.

EL CASTILLO (the castle) at the Mayan City of Chichén Itzá is one of the most impressive structures in Yucatán. Composed of nine platforms diminishing in size as they rise seventy-five feet in height, the pyramid has a stairway on each side leading to the temple on top. This temple is adorned with relief carvings of the Toltec period beginning around the tenth century A.D., when the Toltecs of Tula, Hidalgo, imposed their religious and artistic ways upon the Mayas at Chichén Itzá. The Toltecs introduced many stylistic innovations — colonnaded galleries, carved pillars, decorative balustrades and semi-crenelated walls, to mention a few — which reflected a fiercer way of life than the Mayan. Geometric details and the number of steps in the castle stairs can be worked out to coincide with the days of the solar year, implying a connection with sun worship. Early records of Catholic priests identify *El Castillo* as the site sacred to Kukulkan, the Mayan name for Quetzalcóatl, the feathered serpent introduced to Yucatán by the Toltecs.

The sculpture below came from another famous Mayan site, Uxmal. It shows a priest, or perhaps a god, emerging from the mouth of a serpent.

The pre-Hispanic city of Tula was reduced to ruins near the end of the twelfth century A.D. Since the area was partly abandoned by then, the invaders — perhaps the Chichimecs — found the city an easy prey. Rediscovered in 1940, the pyramids, palaces and ball courts are extremely difficult to restore. Pyramid "B" is shown on the opposite page. Fronted by a colonnaded hall, the platform on the inside of the lowest parapet was decorated with polychromed bas-reliefs. In the last centuries of its existence Tula was dominated by the military, who deposed the priest-king Topíltzin, a pacifist. The decorations are consequently more secular than religious. At right is one of the atlantean figures that supported the roof of the temple. These sculptures represent warriors. On the opposite page, at the bottom, is a detail showing relief carving from another column.

BELOW: The serpent wall, decorated with friezes, shows in relief a serpent eating a human. The head, reduced to a skull, can be identified at the right end of the main panel. OPPOSITE: (*Above*) This composite head, probably representing Quetzalcóatl, is a detail from the relief carvings that decorated the four sides of the base of Pyramid "B." (*Below*) Another view of one of the colossi.

Mexico's pre-Hispanic deities tend to have tongue-twisting names and multifarious representations. For example, the incarnate form of Quetzalcóatl (feathered serpent) was varied, one of the most interesting being Tlahuizcalpantecuhtli (or morning star). These ancient gods never yielded entirely to Christianity. And then, of course, Cortés himself was thought to be Topíltzin Quetzalcóatl, the deposed priest from Tula, who was said to have sailed away on a raft of serpents into the Gulf of Mexico five centuries earlier. Topíltzin's promised return was still anticipated by Moctezuma.

To the natives of polytheistic pre-Columbian Mexico, accepting the personages central to Christianity was not difficult. Christ was quickly identified with the sun, the Virgin Mary with the moon. The Chamulas in the state of Chiapas still believe that the sun was once cold like the moon but was ignited with fire and life-giving heat at Christ's birth. Further, it seems natural, even witty, that an archangel with his trumpet should become a patron saint of musicians. The outcome is that pre-Hispanic symbols often figure in architectural embellishments, even though their original meanings may be lost in time. The moon in a church now signifies the entrance of the Virgin into the world.

OPPOSITE: (*Top*) The ubiquitous god Quetzalcóatl shown here is from the base of a pyramid at Teotihuacan. This structure is older than the less ornate Pyramids of the Sun and the Moon. (*Below*) The awesome goddess of terrestrial waters, Chalchiuhtlicue, was photographed in the National Museum of Anthropology. RIGHT: One of the most famous and exigent of the pre-Hispanic deities, Tlaloc, god of the rain.

The great Pyramid of the Sun at Teotihuacan had this general shape when the local culture was flourishing between the fourth and ninth centuries A.D. Experts are still unable to decide what peoples built this ancient city and what happened to them when they left. The Aztecs, who were in power when Cortés arrived, seem to have been just as mystified by Teotihuacan. Below appears a modern representation of the sun.

Mexico's Ministry of Foreign Relations, above, stands near the spot where Cuauhtemoc surrendered Mexico to Hernán Cortés, August 13, 1521. The marble façade of the Ministry is elegantly simple; its floor plans are highly functional. Both features contribute to the dignity and efficiency of this governmental department. Located on the edge of the Tlatelolco district, the building was designed by Pedro Ramírez Vásquez and Rafael Mijares A., with the collaboration of Bernardo Uribe, Arturo Ayala and Victor Lara.

The Franciscans, who began to arrive in Mexico in 1523, soon built the Church of Santiago, shown in profile at left above (see frontispiece for another view). Building material was the stone taken from the two great pyramids of Tlatelolco.

The Church of Santiago has been considerably restored because it was to be a focal point in the Plaza of Three Cultures (i.e., pre-Hispanic, colonial and modern) in the new Tlatelolco. The interior of the church, shown below, was renovated under the direction of Ricardo de Robina. On the opposite page, bottom, is another interior view showing one of the many windows designed by Mathias Goeritz.

BELOW: The modern confessional for the Church of Santiago, designed by de Robina. OPPOSITE PAGE: At top is one of the modern stations of the cross, designed by Goeritz. Below is the baroque baptistry.

Although Cortés conquered in the name of Spain the conquest that followed was primarily the Church's. At no time in recorded history has architecture played a greater role in the promulgation of a new culture. Existing religious structures were often razed, usually providing building materials for the new order. At Cholula alone, some 300 churches were built on top of sites sacred to the Toltecs. Thus architecture brilliantly symbolized the demise of one religious order and the establishment of another. For this reason, we repeat, any treatise dealing with Mexican architecture must become largely and inextricably involved with the religious buildings themselves. Still profoundly involved in religion today, Mexico continues to produce a host of churches, many of them significant as architecture.

OPPOSITE PAGE: The Church of San Agustín in Acolman, in the State of Mexico. The Augustinian friars came to Mexico in 1533 and formed a settlement at Acolman in 1539. This church, dated 1560, is a fine example of the sumptuousness which this order of friars brought to Mexican architecture. The fine plateresque façade has an elegant representation of the annunciation. St. Peter and St. Paul occupy the niches.

ABOVE: Decorative details from Acolman show some of early Mexico's finest high-relief carving. OPPOSITE PAGE: Details showing St. Peter. Figure above with basket on head represents fecundity. The St. Gabriel at right is part of the annunciation scene.

The early-seventeenth-century building shown on the opposite page is the Capilla de Don Vasco de Quiroga. Located not far from Pátzcuaro, in the state of Michoacan, it honored the bishop and great humanitarian, Quiroga, but in later centuries has also been known in the Spanish vernacular as the Church of Cristo del Humilladero. The relief carving on the façade is especially fine, having been done with restraint and impeccable taste. Of special interest is the decorative detail in the pediment over the door, shown close-up on page 61.

ABOVE: Detail from the Capilla de Don Vasco de Quiroga, showing pre-Hispanic sun and moon with symbols of the crucifixion. OPPOSITE PAGE: The cross mounted in the open atrium bears the date of 1628. Early architects did not show Christ crucified because the representation confused the new converts.

LEFT: The Cathedral of Zacatecas stands in such a narrow street that the façade in its entirety can be shown only with distortion, which results from photographing with a wide-angle lens. BELOW: Sculptures representing St. Paul and St. Peter.

Above: The large figures are the four evangelists. Notice the small figure of Christ holding the world in his hands.

The Cathedral of Zacatecas began as a parish church in 1579. The elaborate façade and main structure were designed in the seventeenth century, but not finished until 1752. This is probably Mexico's best example of baroque Solomonic architecture.

Remarkable detail above from the Cathedral at Zacatecas is reminiscent of a medieval rose window. The large figures, the doctors of the church, from left to right, top to bottom, are St. Ambrose, St. Jerome, St. Augustine and St. John Chrysostom. Just above the keystone is a symbol of the Eucharist. The wrought-iron grill has an asymmetrical representation of the pre-Hispanic sun and moon.

Main portal of the Cathedral of Zacatecas. Small figure above keystone is the Virgin of Guadalupe crowned.

OPPOSITE PAGE: (*Left*) In Guadalajara, a life-size St. Christopher stands high in a niche carved into a corner of the Church of Santa Monica. (*Right*) A detail showing St. Francis in the Guadalajara Church of San Felipe, one of the oldest in that city. ABOVE: Also from San Felipe in Guadalajara. The center tablet shows the assumption of the Virgin. Smaller tablet at left shows the Holy Trinity, while the tablet at right probably represents the education of the Virgin. The San Felipe façade is an excellent example of early eclecticism in Mexican architecture.

The basilica at Zapopan, Jalisco, is one of the most holy in Mexico. As it stands today, the building is not very old but it is interesting architecturally because it represents a sort of ultimate in the eclecticism that blended most of the styles imported from Europe.

The building housing the University of Puebla was once a huge religious complex adjoining a Dominican church. The salon (*Above*) was one of the many chapels, all with churrigueresque ceilings. OPPOSITE PAGE: A relief carving in wood from an end chair in the choir.

On these two pages are more details from the churrigueresque salon at the University of Puebla.

The eighteenth-century baroque style which flourished in the state of Puebla is unique for several reasons. For one thing, its pattern was nearly always rigidly European, admitting almost nothing indigenous to pre-Hispanic Mexico. The use of tile is Moorish, of course. Puebla had been an important ceramic center in pre-Hispanic days, however, so that borrowing this Moorish-Spanish architectural habit must have seemed especially congenial to the Pueblans.

The Church of San Francisco Acatepec, on the opposite page, is a good example of Puebla baroque. Even the columns are faced with mosaic. But the interior, shown on the four pages which follow, illustrates a baroque churrigueresque that is especially interesting because it uses a few pre-Hispanic symbols. Similar symbols are much more in evidence in the Church of Santa María Tonantzintla, not far from Acatepec.

LEFT: Baroque confessional of San Francisco Acatepec. BELOW: These little Puebla angels are typical of the Puebla style. OPPOSITE PAGE: Other interior details.

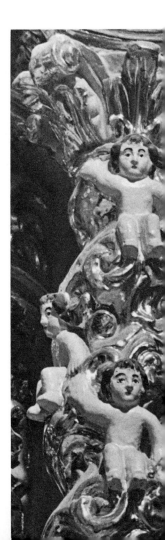

RIGHT: A happy golden sun is a pre-Hispanic vestige.
BELOW: More cherubs in the Puebla style.

Details from the ceiling at San Francisco Acatepec, featuring a tablet showing the annunciation.

The village of Tlalmanalco is situated high in the mountains not far from the volcano Popocatépetl. As shown on these pages, the central church has a high altar of considerable splendor.

RIGHT: The relief at the top shows the visitation of St. Elizabeth to St. Anne. The large carved figures — the *old* ones — are, from left to right, top to bottom, St. Francis, St. John the Baptist, St. Anthony, St. John the Evangelist, St. Peter, St. Joaquin, St. Anne and St. Paul. The Virgin and the Christ are inferior carvings of a later period. BELOW: Detail showing St. Anne and St. Paul.

The sanctuary of the Virgin at Ocotlán is located on a hill overlooking the city of Tlaxcala. The intricate decorations on the façade are actually a refined type of rubblework (*mampostería*) in which the final design is realized by applying plaster over a basic, generalized shape in brick or pieces of stone rubble. The late Manuel Toussaint classed this particular façade as "popular art." When the plaster has received its annual coat of whitewash, the resulting fantasy might have come from a pastry tube.

The Tlaxcaltecs surrendered peacefully to Cortés on September 23, 1519. Their area in Mexico was the first missionary center for the friars arriving from Spain. The architecture shown here, however, is clearly eighteenth century. The clay tile, juxtaposed with white plaster, is an adaptation of the style that flourished in the neighboring state of Puebla.

ABOVE: Framed by a star window, the Immaculate Virgin stands on the three worlds resting on the shoulders of St. Francis. RIGHT: An archangel.

The style of this church in Amayuca, Morelos, might be described as naive baroque. Its façade and interior decoration are typical of the charming work of local artisans in the central highlands of Mexico. The anonymous designer of this particular façade has unknowingly wandered into the stylistic domain of Henry Moore. The St. Michael (right), like the rest of the façade, was once painted white and still bears traces of accents in blue and pink.

LEFT: Detail, showing St. Peter from the façade at Amayuca. BELOW: St. Augustine, Bishop of Hippo, with his miter askew, is part of the ceiling decorations at Amayuca. The style recalls that of the popular *retablos,* usually painted on tin.

Authorities in Puebla recently began an impressive program
that will eventually refurbish all the city's churches and restore
those of particular importance. Shown above, from the Church
of St. Christopher, is a side portal which had been hidden
under plaster a few centuries ago. On the opposite page is a
detail, showing the keystone with its ingenuous Puebla-style
angel bearing the moon on its shoulders. Notice the sun above
the cornice.

Carving of great elegance decorates the pediment of a side portal of
the monastery at Tepotzotlan. Like the church itself (page 19), these
buildings will eventually be restored.

Moorish Gothic seems the only term for these ceramac-tiled domes
of the church at Huajuapan de León, in the state of Oaxaca.

There is no end of surprising details in Mexico's religious architecture. ABOVE: Caryatids flank the oculus in the massive façade of Puebla's Church of St. Peter. The Ionic style was never much in vogue in Mexico. OPPOSITE PAGE: (*Top*) What might have been the torus, or upper half of the base of a column, has grown here in typical churrigueresque abandon until it forms nearly a fourth of the column itself. From a church in Oaxaca. (*Center*) Carved detail from the thick wooden door in the main portal of the Church of St. Peter (c. 1602) at Zacatlán, in the northern part of the state of Puebla. (*Bottom*) From Xochimilco, this startling detail shows what may be a pre-Hispanic god of death fixed into the wall behind a font. The juxtaposition is intended to symbolize the death of paganism and the birth of Christianity.

Clearly inspired by Murillo, this small sculpture (about 32 inches tall) stands in the open atrium of the Church of St. Peter in Zacatlán, Puebla

LEFT: Protector of animals, most especially dogs, the Spanish St. Roque stands high in the niche of a former church in Puebla. Over four feet tall, he is of polychromed wood. BELOW: Patio of the tiles, once an exercise yard for the adjoining monastery. Notice the intricate use of ceramic tile in the balustrade. This important courtyard will be restored when funds are available.

When the friars began building their churches in Mexico, the architecture served first of all as a means of promoting Christianity. In other words, the designs were often teaching devices. For example, the façade at Acolman shows an annunciation carved above its main portal. Painting of the churches' interiors was more explicit. It depicted not only episodes from the lives of the saints but also Mexican Indians being converted to Rome. In the years that followed, the successful conversion of Mexico eliminated the early role that architecture had placed.

Free of its task as teacher, architecture became more ebullient. In the mid-seventeenth century medieval styles gave way to baroque, which persisted with ever-growing exuberance into the nineteenth century, when neo-classicism appeared in Mexico. Cold and formal, it is a style that implies power and permanence. This manner began to dwindle when Maximilian and Carlotta came to Mexico but often survived as a detail in the eclecticism that embraced a bit of everything during the reign of Porfirio Díaz.

Shown here is the neo-classical Church of the Virgen del Carmen in Celaya. Though actually a renovation, completed in 1807, of an earlier church destroyed by fire, it is considered one of the best works by architect Francisco Eduardo Tresguerras (1759-1833), an indefatigable native of Celaya who excelled in all the arts.

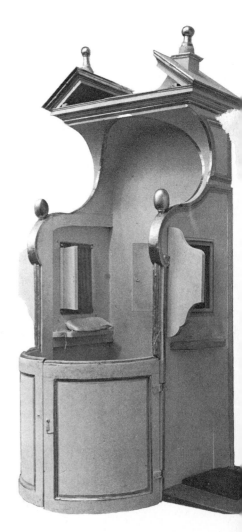

Other interior details from the Tresguerras Church of the Virgen del Carmen.

OPPOSITE PAGE: An interior view of the Cathedral of Cuernavaca, which has been abuilding since 1529. Its present state — which cannot be described as static — is due mostly to the influence of Monsignor Sergio Méndez Arceo, eleventh bishop of Cuernavaca, who is shown above. Fascinating, highly controversial and often given to wearing psychedelic vestments at public benedictions, this important prelate has been outspoken in his conviction that religious architecture must serve the aims of the living church rather than produce museum pieces or confect "specimens" of architecture.

AT RIGHT: One of the many modern windows designed by Mathias Goeritz for the Cathedral at Cuernavaca.

What is the direction of religious architecture in Mexico today? The demand for more buildings is endless but the client is carefully bound by a tradition only recently beginning to admit the innovations and experimentations that modern architects are proffering. Most of the churches play it safe. On the opposite page, upper, is a typical small chapel being built at Ventura, a village in the northern part of the state of San Luis Potosí. It is very much a community project in design as well as finance and labor. Below is a modern church being built in Guadalajara by Enrique de la Mora, an important architect who has done much to change the church's mind about contemporary design. Below on this page is another modern chapel in Mexico City.

The Church of Santa Monica in Mexico City was designed by Fernando López in collaboration with Felix Candela. Candela's imaginative engineering has come to be recognized as an independent art form; its beauty, which begins with logic and function, has had broad technical effect on the production of public buildings throughout the country and abroad.

On these pages are three more interior views of the Church of Santa Monica. At right is the "minimal confessional."

Two interior views of Candela's Church of the Virgen Milagrosa in Mexico City. The raw cement retains the texture of its wooden forms. Though decoration is minimal, the atmosphere is Gothic.

The Maguen-David Synagogue (interior view shown on opposite page) in Mexico City is the work of several designers, including David Serur, Guillermo Hume, Mathias Goeritz and Julian Farah. There are few synagogues in Mexico — the first was built in 1932 — and this one is by far the most interesting architecturally. The confluence of its design elements results in what Goeritz strives to achieve in any project: a "place," an atmosphere, an ambience agreeable to the persons being contained within the structure.

In Mexico City, a small private chapel designed by Juan Sordo Madaleno.

WALLS AND FENCES

The ornamental iron fence which surrounds the cathedral yard in Puebla.

Above: A fence of cast cement at the Aztec Stadium in Mexico City.
Left: A cactus fence in the village of Atotonilco, Morelos.

In Mexico the fence as it exists today was unknown in pre-Hispanic times. The Spaniards introduced it into Mexico. Obviously fences and walls can provide security and satisfy the psychological need to feel "enclosed" but in rural Mexico they may simply define a property line or discourage the wandering of cattle. Architecturally, building a fence can also invite a Mexican to express his innate sense of fancy.

The fences on these two pages are modern in the sense that they were built not very long ago but the materials and the way they are put together are pre-Hispanic. As will be shown later, the pre-Hispanic Mexican probably lived in houses which were distant relatives of the fences shown here.

The four fences shown on these pages are structures which grew. They are esthetically successful examples of architecture produced without an architect. They were photographed in the northern and western deserts, where growing one's own fence is also an economic advantage.

ABOVE: A fence made of large rubble without mortar. OPPOSITE PAGE: A wall in Oaxaca in which the mason carefully emphasized the altitude of his structure by letting the large stones seem to settle at the bottom. BELOW: One of the endless — and attractive — variations that result when a native mason is left to improvise his own design. This fence is made of clay tile.

MEXICAN FANCY

IN every endeavor the Mexican is mindful of certain esthetic considerations. Whatever the task — whether building a big hotel in Acapulco or displaying turnips in a sidewalk market — the result is bound to be affected by the Mexican's sense of color, his strong feeling for texture and form and the effects which light will have upon his creation.

Opposite Page: (*Above*) A cast-iron fence takes its shape from mountains in the background. From the abandoned city of Real de Catorce, San Luis Potosí. (*Below*) A fence of split bamboo, from the fishing village of Tecolutla in Veracruz. Below: A decorative fence from Anenehuilco, Morelos.

OPPOSITE PAGE: Façade of the office at the Hotel Termas Balneario in Atotonilco, Morelos. An abundance of skilled labor can produce decorations like these, where each cement "plank" was individually molded to size and fitted into place. RIGHT: Several Latin countries, especially Portugal and Brazil, are known for their use of molded cement tile that has been colored during the mixing process. This walk, in orange and blue, is from the plaza in Tecōlutla, Vera-cruz.

The fantasy on these two pages is not so grand as the Watts Towers in Los Angeles but it is more delightfully naive and, depending on one's point of view, more amusing. Only recently confected in the state of Tlaxcala, the buildings were intended as a museum to house memorabilia related to Cortés, who enjoyed his first military successes not far away. The monument seems no less than he deserves.

Architect David Muñoz used tiny windows of vary-
ing sizes in the lobby of the Motel Siesta in the country not far from San Miguel de Allende. While the
original idea may have been Arabian, the result here
is purely Mexican. Opposite is a fireplace in the popular Mexican style but with a contemporary effect,
in one of the Siesta's guest rooms.

126 THE ARCHITECTURE OF MEXICO

In the hills near Valenciana, the Hotel Guanajuato dominates a plateau facing the valley of the city of Guanajuato. The skies and the light in this region are justly famous.

Opposite Page: A passage in which changing light induces architectural variations throughout the day. Above: Another view, showing the domed roofs (*bóvedas*) indigenous to the area.

OPPOSITE PAGE: A nuns' window from the convent Dominico de Santiago Apostol, at Cuilpan, Oaxaca. Begun in 1555 but never finished, this famous Gothic building was designed by Antonio de Barbosa. The detail shown here has many variations, some of which appeared in secular architecture.

ABOVE: Detail from an apartment being constructed on top of a building in downtown Mexico City. High walls surround a court which is actually an extension of the bedroom. Privacy, a sense of being enclosed and a feeling of spaciousness have all been attained, but the only modern materials used are the iron frames for the windows. For another view of this apartment, see page 255.

Since water is a basic resource dispensed by special gods in ancient Mexico, its presence and its use inspire a multitude of architectural effects.

ABOVE: One of several amusing drain spouts on a building that houses a cantina near Tlacolula, Oaxaca. BELOW: Water well, with an elegant wrought-iron structure to support the pulley, in the garden of the Casa Mina in Valenciana, Guanajuato. The Casa Mina was built in the late eighteenth century as a residence for the Counts of Valenciana.

Two of the many public water taps in Guanajuato.

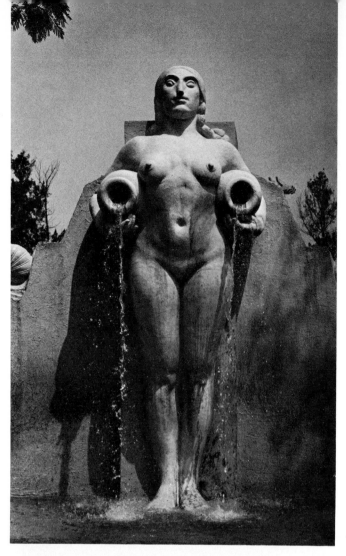

LEFT: Water fountain in the Parque México in Mexico City. The style was popular in the late twenties and early thirties. BELOW: A splendid colonial fountain in the courtyard of the Palace of Justice, Puebla. OPPOSITE PAGE: Fountains in the plaza fronting the cathedral in Guadalajara. At bottom, fountains in a new plaza recently designed by Julio de la Peña in Guadalajara.

The great fountain in the main court of the National Museum of Anthropology in Mexico City.

Designed and produced under the direction of Pedro Ramírez Vásquez, this complex of buildings is one of the most satisfying in modern Mexico. Functionally, the museum itself is an incomparable example of institutional architecture. Four great buildings join to form the court shown here, nearly half of it sheltered by a huge aluminum umbrella supported by a stone-faced column. Water, used as an important design element, splashes down the column to a recessed pond below.

RIGHT: Detail of the carved column that supports the aluminum umbrella sheltering part of the great court in the National Museum of Anthropology. ABOVE: Another view of the court, conveying the grandeur of scale everywhere evident in the museum.

Another view, from the opposite end of
the inner court at the museum, showing
all of the giant fountain with its aluminum
canopy.

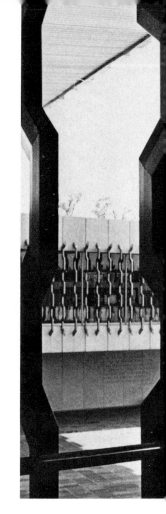

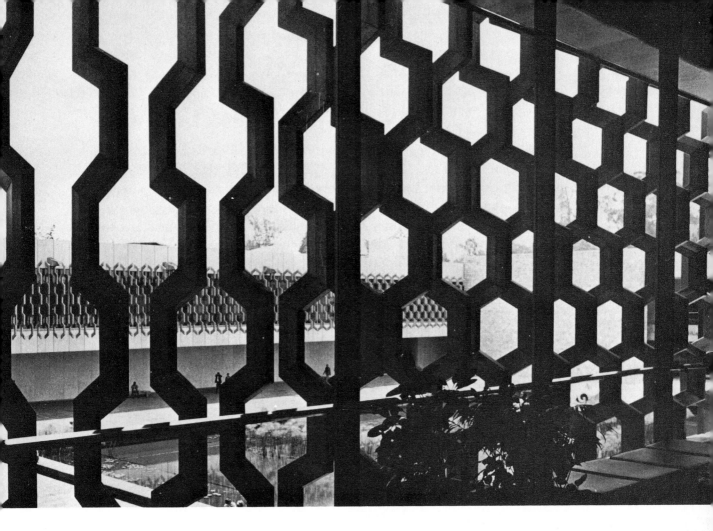

Two views showing façades and their details, facing the great court in the museum.

When they designed the Automex Factory in Toluca, Ricardo Legorreta and his associates brushed aside many conventional ideas that have plagued industrial architecture. Legorreta planned a community in which extreme functionalism meshes happily with art. The lesson has not been wasted in Mexico, where modern industry no longer considers it frivolous or flashy to be esthetic. In every part of the country industrialists are discovering that efficiency reports and production programs can be pleasantly influenced by a carefully designed and maintained environment.

The Toluca project is a prime example of Legorreta's superb organizational ability. In Mexico, it amounts to a special kind of genius. While delegating authority to a gifted and distinguished staff, he is still able to produce works which show the unmistakable and fastidious taste of the architect himself.

Although Legorreta's expression is not provincial and is certainly of the twentieth century, it is native, revealing again the Mexican's feeling for the monumental, his innate and usually infallible sense of design and his predilection for forms and textures.

Two huge cones with flat tops sit in a court to form a focal point of the factory complex but their function has recently become more than decorative. Both of the towers now contain water tanks and the big one also houses an auditorium. These spectacular structures have become a dramatic symbol of the entire complex. They were designed for Legorreta by Mathias Goeritz.

The eye is led by diminishing perspectives to pleasant terminal points throughout the Automex Factory. The façade shown here conceals the administrative offices, which face a grassy lawn of some two square acres. Detailing in the façade, using the movement of light as a secondary architectural element, is characteristic of Legoretta's work.

Another façade in the Automex Factory with protruding beams forming secondary designs on the plaster walls as the light changes.

Two more views of the Automex plant showing, again, how perspective, as an intangible design element, leads the eye pleasantly over basic forms and textures that become decorative as well as functional.

Achieving the monumental in Mexican architecture is a part of that country's heritage. It began with the great pyramids. As Mexico reasserts its identity, a process that has involved revolutions and an inexorable plunge into the age of technology, a feeling for the monumental remains intact and flourishing.

Though an eminently functional structure, the Aztec Stadium, shown on these pages, may be enjoyed at the same time as pure architecture. Not a small part of its beauty stems from the mathematical niceties that control its function as a structure. Architectural engineering must derive its esthetics from Euclid but when the application is Mexican the consequence is bound to be colored by native instincts.

Left: An interior view of the stadium, showing the spectacular aluminum awning that shelters the stands. Above: A telephoto view of the stadium's exterior showing how its structural members create a unifying design made from cement and steel. Architects were Pedro Ramírez Vásquez and Rafael Mijares A., with Luis Martínez del Campo as supervising architect.

Parts of the Aztec Stadium
seen as pure sculpture.

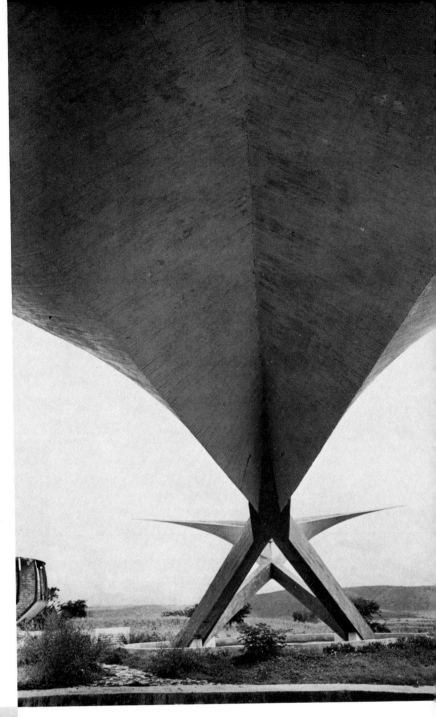

This decorative fantasy is a startling piece of sculpture at the entrance of a small resort on the shores of Lake Tequesquitengo in the state of Morelos. It was designed by Guillermo Rosell and Manuel Larrosa but owes its realization to the imaginative engineering of Felix Candela. As in much of Candela's work, thin membranes of raw cement are mathematically curved to be self-supporting. An attractive innovation here is the steel base, which lets the two opposing design elements pit their weight against each other.

AN OLD CITY

R EAL de Catorce, a village in the northern part of the state of San Luis
Potosí, came into existence in the late eighteenth century. Like Zacatecas, Taxco and Guanajuato, it began as a mining town — at one time it
had approximately 25,000 inhabitants — but after the revolution of 1910 it
faded into obscurity and today is abandoned. Almost inaccessible, it is situated at more than 9000 feet in the mountains above the desert floor west of
Matehuala. Though the city was looted during the revolution and has since
fallen prey to unscrupulous "builders" and antique dealers who have pil-
fered much of its decorative ornamentations, it still has the air of an early-
nineteenth-century city which became frozen in time.

Architecturally, Real de Catorce is a cross-section of the period between
1777, when city records were begun by a local priest, and 1910, when ban-
dits began to loot the city. At the beginning, wealth created by the mines
attracted citizens of aristocratic taste. They preferred a restrained Palladian
style with some elaboration borrowed from the baroque, avoiding the in-
flexible formality of neo-classicism. Though fun-loving, these people insisted
on opulence too, so long as it was not too formal. Their architects are yet to
be discovered. Their special European tastes were also influential in the city
of San Luis Potosí, the financial headquarters for the mines of the area.

OPPOSITE PAGE: Carved stone dolphin heads form part of the beams supporting
the narrow stone floor of this balcony. The two windows are eclectic but restrained. Of particular interest is the wrought iron, tastefully embellished with a
tied-bow motif, dating the house in the earliest part of the nineteenth century.

ABOVE: The main public fountain of Real de Catorce is a series of circles set into a steep incline paved with hand-cut stone. All the streets are paved with this material, much of it flint. In some areas a geometric design emerges, thanks partly to the shape of the stones and partly to their differences in color. LEFT: A fuel-burning lamp. It had been taken down by vandals, but is now reinstalled by its owner, one of the approximately 125 people now living in Catorce.

Above: The Casa de la Moneda, where federal money was minted shortly before the revolution of 1910. The magnificent portal faces the church and plaza, which opens onto steeply inclined streets and mountain views reminiscent of Taxco and Guanajuato. Left: Carved detail from the door shown above.

OPPOSITE PAGE: A pseudo-Palladian portal from what was once a hacienda not far from Catorce. ABOVE: Second-floor detail of one of the best-preserved houses in Catorce. Notice the fretted relief set below the cornice and the absolutely simple wrought iron of the balcony.

ABOVE: The disintegration of taste in the late nineteenth century was somewhat vitiated by humor, as in the cast-iron lighting fixture above, one of several used to decorate a plaza. LEFT: A padlock, probably English, still in use. Antique dealers have divested Catorce of much of its hardware.

Handmade nails, more than a century old, make
black designs in the wood of a weathered door.

Above: Cast iron, at Real de Catorce, appeared later in the nineteenth century to satisfy the increased demand for ornamentation. By then Catorce was among the three largest producers of silver in the republic. Left: Anticipating art nouveau, these cast-iron benches at Catorce must have been sold by a peddler who visited all the rich mining cities of the period. Identical benches were once installed in the plaza of silver-rich Valenciana, in the state of Guanajuato.

Cast iron on another balcony in Real de Catorce. Notice that the beams are of wood, not stone, and that the floor, which must have been of wood, no longer exists.

THE CHANGING CITY

Lᴜᴋᴇ several cities of the period, San Miguel is a national monument and not allowed to change. On occasion some concession may be made, as in Querétaro, where extensive and successful renovation included the removal of cobblestones to be replaced by unglazed clay tile, a more "sympathetic" paving for automobile traffic. But in other places (below) like Mexico City or Monterrey or Guadalajara, what is new must be geared to the country's quickened pace. Multi-layered housing, for example, seems alien to the traditional manner of living in Mexico but now there is no turning back. Mexico City alone will soon have a population of 8,000,000. Architects and city planners are making frantic efforts to cope with the effects of this population explosion. On the six pages which follow are some notable examples of the institutional architecture that has begun to change the city's character.

Oᴘᴘᴏsɪᴛᴇ Pᴀɢᴇ: One of the main streets in San Miguel de Allende, Guanajuato.

ABOVE: Mexico City's stock exchange was renovated to meet the pace of modern investment. The architect was Enrique de la Mora, in collaboration with Felix Candela and Leonardo Zeevaert. OPPOSITE PAGE: The Hotel María Isabel in Mexico City exemplifies the de luxe accommodations in an international style being built all over the country to meet the demand of travelers. Newly affluent, the Mexicans form a large part of the clientele. The architect was Juan Sordo Madaleno, his collaborator José Villagrán García.

ABOVE: The so-called "hanging office building" in Monterrey, designed for the Monterrey Insurance Company by Enrique de la Mora in collaboration with Alberto González Pozo and Leonardo Zeevaert. OPPOSITE PAGE: Augusto H. Alvarez designed the Cedulas Hipotecarios Building on Mexico City's Paseo de la Reforma.

On these two pages are views of a small but highly original office building on Praga Street in Mexico City. Completed in early 1968, it is the work of a young architect, Agustín Hernández.

PRE-HISPANIC VESTIGES

IN THE MEXICAN HOUSE

IN Mexico as early as 1000 B.C. the building techniques of pole-and-thatch and wattle-and-daub were in use. Variations of this technique survive in several parts of the world where primitive societies once flourished. Since the architectural design results from the building's utility, form can be said to have followed function long before the expression became a dictum. Of course the climate has exerted its influence on design — and still does where so-called popular Mexican architecture flourishes.

Shown on this page are two buildings from Atotonilco, Morelos. Both have similar roofs, but the one in the foreground uses a sophisticated technique with rubble and poles for the walls. The other structure uses adobe, a modern relative of wattle-and-daub.

OPPOSITE PAGE: (*Bottom*) A model from the National Museum of Anthropology showing a typical yard and house built in part with pre-Hispanic techniques. (*Above*) A minimal shelter from a hot, humid climate near the Tecolutla River in Veracruz. BELOW: An ancient type of *troje*, or granary (see also page 26) built in part with the wattle-and-daub technique. This highly functional shape expands from the base, making it nearly impossible for rodents to climb up and rob the grain. In function, building technique and design, variations of this *troje* appear in many parts of the world, most notably near the Volta River on the Ivory Coast.

In wooded areas a house like this is possible. The hip roof is of palm leaves, which function well in the northern mountains of Oaxaca, where there is much rainfall.

In more desert areas, where both wood and palm are scarce, adobe is the popular building material. A shed roof, made of clay tile, suffices here, in the state of Coahuila, where there is little rain. Tile and adobe also offer insulation against the heat.

HOUSES OLD AND NEW

OPPOSITE PAGE: (*Above*) An adobe house with
fine hip roof. When he becomes a bit more well-
to-do the owner may plaster the walls, as in the
flat-roofed house (*below*). BELOW: An unusual
house of board-and-batten in the tropical area of
Veracruz. RIGHT: Detail showing how the builder
encouraged natural ventilation by leaving the
soffit open to allow warm air to escape as it col-
lects near the ceiling.

Details from the village of Tingüindin, Michoacan. A brisk climate, especially at night, and a brilliant sun in the day suggest the need for thick walls, shuttered windows and wide overhangs. The design also provides an excuse to carve the supporting beams where they are exposed. The detail at the upper left shows how the interior ceiling was treated in the corner of the house shown below.

RIGHT: Carved stonework set into the corner of a house in Tingüindin. BELOW: Across the country, in the village of Chignahuapan, in the northernmost part of the state of Puebla, occurs another style of popular Mexican architecture. Of particular interest here is the balcony enclosed with pierced wood to give a Moorish effect.

In making frames for doors and windows the Mexican *albañil*, or mason, generally arrives at his own unique design. Even when the same man does them, these forms will vary from job to job. Their scale and decorative value are invariably correct. Professor Willis W. Pratt's house, shown here, was built over ruins on a site near the famous Casa Mina in Valenciana, Guanajuato.

Salvador Macías Contreras' Puebla house, tastefully restored, is an unusual example of the typical residence that can still be seen in all parts of that city. While the façade is faced with a typical alternating pattern of glazed and unglazed tile, the classical molding on the cornices lends an atypical restrained elegance. As a rule, the tiled façades are enlivened with baroque cornices, window frames and portals. The ultimate expression of this baroque combined with tile is the famous *Casa de Alfeñique*, or Sugar-Candy House (not shown in this book), which in its own unique ebullience is also atypical.

Most of the living in the Macías house revolves around this large inner court. Its main decorative feature is the elaborate colonial fountain, obtained from another site.

A very early Puebla house erected when the style was beginning to form. In bad repair today, it nevertheless retains the basic excellence of its design and its fine, simply elegant wrought-iron balconies.

The portal here is much later than the house shown on page 190. *Mampostería*, plaster over rubble, which eventually loses its crispness through erosion, yielded this frivolous but pleasant design. The façade itself is faced in another style in which exposed mortar is left to form a pattern between the unglazed tiles. The mortar, like the plaster surrounding the door, is frequently brightened up with fresh paint.

BELOW: In Mexico City art nouveau is not confined to any particular neighborhood but the architecture in the vicinity of Chihuahua and Frontera streets, where this window was photographed, is particularly interesting. RIGHT: A complete antonym to art nouveau is this fine window from the Hacienda La Cañada, built in 1808, in the state of Hidalgo. It has the quiet dignity and security of a bank.

RIGHT: Many fine examples of nineteenth-century French architecture graced Mexico City where the Colonias Roma and Júarez overlapped. The example shown here, with its carved stone and leaded glass, is in Nápoles Street. BELOW: (*Right*) A detail from the French façade above. (*Left*) French taste went unrestrained during the reign of Porfirio Díaz. This early example, from Oaxaca, uses especially fine relief carving to frame the window.

ABOVE: The window shown here is Moorish in origin but has existed in various forms in Mexico since the nineteenth century. Forming a tiny enclosed porch, it provides light and ventilation but keeps out the rain and direct sun. The concept became increasingly popular during the revolution because the design provided a certain security. A lady who lives in this house remembers that through this window, as a child safe from bullets, she watched Emiliano Zapata "swaggering in the street." OPPOSITE PAGE: An early colonial window in a house in the village of Santa María del Río, San Luis Potosí. This classical shell was sacred to Santiago and has been immensely popular in secular architecture, too.

This window is from a once-grand country residence at Potrero, not far from the abandoned city of Real de Catorce, San Luis Potosí. Dating from approximately 1805, it has a perfectly scaled false gable terminating in a Palladian finial. The classically fretted cornice and the simple wrought-iron grill are further examples of the restrained taste which aristocratic Spaniards brought from Europe during this period.

An eclectic window from
San Miguel de Allende, Guanajuato.

If he has perseverance, acumen and means, the prospective builder can create an "old" house from vintage materials and still have a house with all the contemporary conveniences. Is this procedure valid architecturally? Most modern architects are apt to say no but the clients who propose to live in such houses seem untroubled by abstract esthetic considerations.

The pickings are rich in Mexico. Gothic columns, sculptured cornices, whole portals, colonial fountains, fanciful keystones and a plethora of related materials can be had if the timing is right. Demolition experts base their bids on the quantity and quality of the stonework. Nowadays in Mexico City there are at least two small new suburbs built almost wholly from the exquisite scraps of old buildings.

Two Puebla houses here illustrate the trend. OPPOSITE PAGE: The new house of Mr. and Mrs. Marco Aurelio Barocio has a carriage entrance with old doors framed in carved stone from an early-nineteenth-century structure. BELOW: The side entrance is a design of direct colonial simplicity.

The best part of a colonial fountain was reassembled to make an impressive planter in the entrance court of the Barocio house.

ABOVE: Domed ceiling in the entrance hall of the Barocio house. BELOW: An unusually fine example of Mexican baroque furniture, originally used in a church choir.

OPPOSITE PAGE: (*Above*) Vaulted ceiling in dining room was constructed by artisans from Guanajuato. (*Below*) Second-floor study has beams and carved columns in the straightforward style of popular Mexican architecture. RIGHT: A stone lion in the garden guards the house against evil spirits. BELOW: A view of the patio. The colonial fountain is a reproduction but the window and its grill came from an old house in Oaxaca.

ABOVE: The semi-enclosed garden in the Puebla home of Mr. and Mrs. Enrique Estrada. The columns are authentic; some of the beams are reproductions. OPPOSITE PAGE: A view from the patio shown above, with its fine colonial fountain and the snow-capped volcano Popocatépetl in the distance. Notice the mitered tile paving in the patio.

In Marfil, the once-opulent suburb of the city of Guanajuato, many of the ruins connected with the early mining industry have become houses of spectacular scale and grandeur. What makes the house appearing on these and the next eight pages unique is that its owners, Dr. and Mrs. Virgilio Fernández, have utilized native techniques in realizing designs which, though modern, still harmonize with the architectural traditions of Guanajuato.

The renovation of this structure began in 1963. Most of the original walls, some of them nearly three feet thick, still serve. Almost all the carved stone for doors and windows is new. Their designs were made by Mrs. Fernández, a Canadian painter and sculptor known professionally as Gene Byron. Under her careful, patient supervision, local craftsmen executed her designs in the pale green-gray stone quarried nearby. The pineapple, a traditional symbol of hospitality, usually adorns the keystones. Flowers and birds assume the same stylized forms, Mexican in their inspiration, to be found in Miss Byron's paintings.

BELOW: A partial view of the house seen from the main entry of the court. OPPOSITE PAGE: One of several impressive doors opening into the main entrance of the house itself. An inside view of this door appears on page 210.

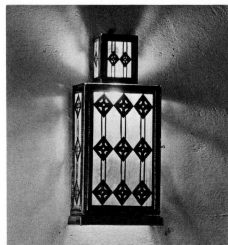

The main living section of the Fernández house is more than seventy feet long. Massive arches supporting the *bóveda*, or domed ceiling, define four principal areas. Building such a ceiling requires a novel and unorthodox local technique. The chased tin lamp (*left*) was designed by Miss Byron.

LEFT: An inside view of the door shown on page 206. BELOW: Huge fireplace carved from native stone by local craftsmen.

Two views of typical windows (these are from the master bathroom) reveal the massive thickness of the walls. The small round window framed by a design of cut stone in the photograph below was a part of the original building.

OPPOSITE PAGE: A view of the dining room. The chased tin candlestick and wall light are of Miss Byron's design. BELOW: The balcony floor of stone slabs rests on carved beams of the same material. RIGHT: The balcony adjoins a deck opening from the master bedroom on the second floor. The arches frame an outdoor sitting room on the ground floor.

ABOVE: In the guest bathroom a washbasin and tile of the same clay and glaze exemplify a popular art form in the Guanajuato area. BELOW: A local craftsman designed and carved these whimsical animals from stone.

The kitchen of popular Mexican architecture accommodates modern appliances.

The Rancho Escolástica, in the state of Querétaro, has served as convent, fort and residence since it was built in the seventeenth century. The present owners, Mr. and Mrs. Pedro Aspe, respect the fine traditional simplicity of the buildings but, as the following pages will show, have combined popular art with period tastes in a country home that is formal and gracious, and comfortable and relaxing at the same time.

ON THESE PAGES: An interior court, with its great colonial fountain, and an intimate garden between the court and the main house. At left is the wrought-iron lamp near the main entry.

These arches frame an outdoor dining terrace opening
onto the lawn and one modern innovation (not visible),
a swimming pool.

The circular main dining room, on the ground floor, has been decorated with painted designs to frame recessed shelves, doors and windows.

ABOVE: All the many bedrooms at Rancho Escolástica have deep windows. This one is whimsically painted to suggest a baroque shell. LEFT: New fireplace in one of the bedrooms is a variation of popular Mexican architecture.

BELOW: Featuring a vanity-desk, another bedroom window opens onto a small private garden. RIGHT: These doors are mounted flush in a plaster wall to conceal a linen closet. Of Puebla origin, the pattern appears to be woven but is actually carved into large sections of wood.

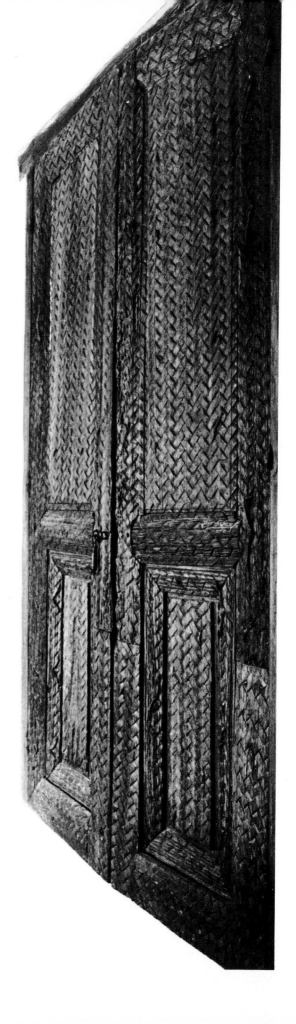

In restoring Rancho Escolástica the owners decided to import Guanajuato craftsmen who could build a domed ceiling, or *bóveda*, for the formal living room. This circular space, some forty feet in diameter, occupies the second floor of the house. No forms support the bricks while the mortar dries. The mason begins at the perimeter, or base, and works around the dome so the bricks are self-supporting even before the last ones are inserted at the pinnacle. The Fernández house (page 209) has domes with rectangular bases. The base of the spectacular ceiling shown here is slightly ellipsoidal.

Enrique Yáñez designed the Mexico City residence on these two pages, a thoroughly modern house allowing for all the exigencies of modern efficient living. Its functionalism has bred design elements that are naturally — perhaps unavoidably — Mexican, however. Protruding beams, pierced tile screening, a supporting arch, iron balustrades and tiled ceilings all serve their intended purpose; yet, esthetically, the effect becomes another expression of the Mexican penchant for forms and textures.

The Yánez house (pages 224-225) is a modern example of functional design where decorative embellishment is a secondary but important result. On these and the four following pages embellishment exists for itself alone. Unlike plateresque, these decorations do not overpower the architecture; they animate and emphasize the volume of a building without seeming to alter its basic form. All photographs were made in Puebla.

OPPOSITE PAGE: (*Bottom*) A late-nineteenth-century door provides a cross-section of the many styles that invaded Mexico — colonial baroque, Palladian and neo-classic. (*Top*) The tile here is highly functional, but its exuberant decorative value does not affect the shape of the bench it covers. The plaster decorations are eclectic. BELOW: One of four brass lions guarding the stair in a Puebla house.

OPPOSITE PAGE: Multicolored glazed tiles adorn the risers in this stair with its carved stone lion to discourage the entry of undesirable spirits. The shaft of the square column and the plinth of its base are also faced with glazed tile. RIGHT: Plaster decorations form an important frame for an otherwise simple window. BELOW: A variation of the quatrefoil window featured in much of Mexico's religious and secular architecture.

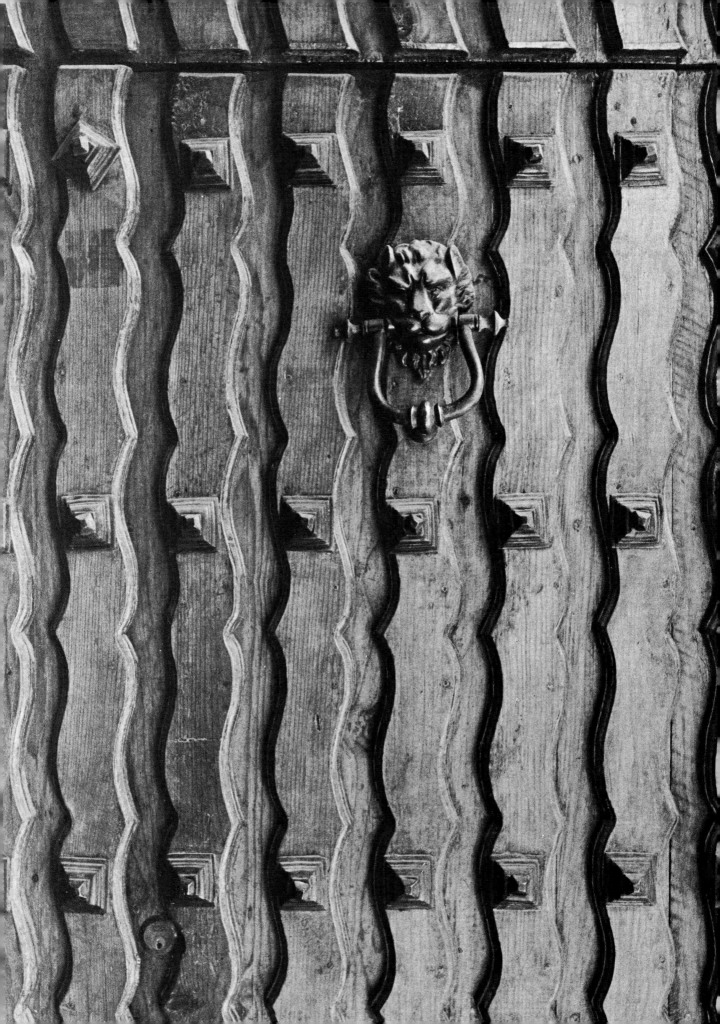

Opposite Page: Fancifully carved battens conceal the straight joints of the structural wood of this door. Notice the symbolic lion's head and the ornamental but functional bosses. Above: A small formal window surrounded by geometrically arranged tile is in curious harmony with a pair of Ionic capitals.

The Hacienda de Lira, south of the village of Pedro Escobedo, Querétaro, is a "working" hacienda, much involved in modern agricultural production. Its lively, discriminating owners, Mr. and Mrs. Carlos Novoa, plan to restore the buildings to their original neo-classical state. Designed by the versatile architect-artist Tresguerras more than a century and a half ago, the hacienda has suffered the whims of various owners who added rooms and neglected the stonework, but the basic plan is still intact.

BELOW: The main façade seen from the outer quadrangle. The second-floor wing at the upper left, with its inferior window, is a later addition. OPPOSITE PAGE: Main portal leading to the inner court connecting the living areas of the house.

ABOVE: Another view of the house seen from the
veranda of the foreman's office. OPPOSITE PAGE:
(*Top*) An elegant window in the main sitting
room. (*Bottom*) One of the windows in the enor-
mous granary. Two goats, sated with food, relax
against the iron grill.

RIGHT: Façade of the house seen from the chapel terrace. OPPOSITE PAGE: Private chapel at the Hacienda de Lira. *Lira* is Spanish for lyre, but "de Lira" here could refer to a type of Spanish poem with a strict meter and rhyme. Its formality would have appealed to architect Tresguerras, who was also at home in the disciplines of music and poetry.

Painted electric blue, this amusing building in
Tecolutla, Veracruz, shows what happens when
a European style invades popular Mexican architecture. The scale and perfect symmetry are
Mexican, the design elements modified Palladian.

The basic form of this Puebla door is identical to the three on the opposite page. Its intricate ornamentation, however, links it with the Porfirian age, the ultimate in opulent frivolity in Mexican architecture.

The Cuernavaca house of Mathias Goeritz. A first cousin to his sculpture and painting, the structure is actually a sort of architectural laboratory where Goeritz jockeys and juxtaposes the basic forms and colors that fascinate him.

BELOW: Two views of the house as seen from the street. The color of the wall and sidewalk depends upon Goerítz' moods. Recently a bright lemon-yellow, it has just changed to an apricot-orange. LEFT: Massive black door seems weightless in its yellow wall.

Two interior views of the Goeritz
house. Notice the Goeritz sculpture in the illuminated niche.

Two views of a free-standing wall in the living room.

The Guanajuato house of Carlo R. Kilp is popular Mexican architecture but the simplicity of its centuries-old style relates it to contemporary design.

A view of the garden at the Kilp house.

A view of the third-floor courtyard designed by Ignacio Díaz for his Guadalajara home.

Living-room wall in the Díaz Morales house.

Detail of shelves invisibly supported by steel straps concealed in
the wall.

Benjamín Méndez designed this recently completed Mexico City house. Though unadorned except for two lighting fixtures, the building's exterior is a series of planes which alter their shapes and textures as the sun moves.

What is it that makes Mexican architecture different? For one thing, esthetic considerations often outweigh practicality: the visual takes precedence. Also, Mexican builders have patience. It is an extraordinary patience. From the most astonishing chaos they can bring order and utility — the upshot is beauty. In the end, architecture is both for and about people. For example, in the small picture here, an early-afternoon sun casts sharp shadows that frame a small country garden and its sparkling fountain. On the opposite page, a private collector in downtown Mexico City has hung his Federico Cantú bronze on a whitewashed wall. The cherub's shadow moves with the sun. In both country garden and city courtyard Mexicans have sought and achieved the visually satisfying. A man-made environment predicated on beauty can only be good.

ACKNOWLEDGMENTS: Many individuals, government agencies and business firms lent friendly assistance in the preparation of this book. For many helpful suggestions I am grateful to Mr. and Mrs. Eduardo Villaseñor, Mr. and Mrs. Fred K. Fries, Alberto Apango Yáñez, Rafael Navarro B. and Professor Thomas M. Cranfill. Reynaldo Velásquez Noriega and José Luis Ibarra Gálvez were the patient, enterprising assistants who helped make the photographs.